PICTURE FACTS

DRAGSTERS

PICTURE FACTS
DRAGSTERS

Norman Barrett

Franklin Watts

London   New York   Sydney   Toronto

Published by:

Franklin Watts
96 Leonard Street
London EC2A 4RH

Franklin Watts Australia
14 Mars Road
Lane Cove
NSW 2066

ISBN: Paperback edition 0 7496 0395 X
        Hardback edition   0 86313 490 4

Copyright © 1987 Franklin Watts

Paperback edition 1990

Hardback edition published
in the Picture Library series.

Printed in Singapore

Designed by
Barrett & Willard

Photographs by
Andy Willsheer
Brian Gibson (Don Garlits Museum picture)

Illustration by
Rhoda & Robert Burns

Technical Consultant
Tony Beadle

Contents

Introduction

Drag racing is a fast and furious motor sport. Cars called dragsters race in pairs on a special quarter-mile (402 m) track, or drag strip. A race lasts for no more than a few seconds. The winner of each race goes through to the next round.

   There are several different types, or classes, of dragsters. Some run on regular petrol. But the fastest use special fuels.

△ Two drag racers approach the start. The noise of their powerful engines revving up is deafening.

The fastest cars are the top-fuellers. Funny cars have fibreglass bodies. Both classes run on a special mixture of nitromethane, a type of rocket fuel. There are also classes for these cars running on alcohol fuel.

Other classes include pro stocks, competition, super stocks and super gas. Jet-powered dragsters and "wheelie" cars sometimes take part in exhibitions.

△ A top-fueller with back wheels spinning and producing clouds of smoke. This is called burnout. It is done before the start of a race to warm up the tyres. Top-fuellers are sometimes known as pro-fuellers or just dragsters.

The dragster

Cockpit view

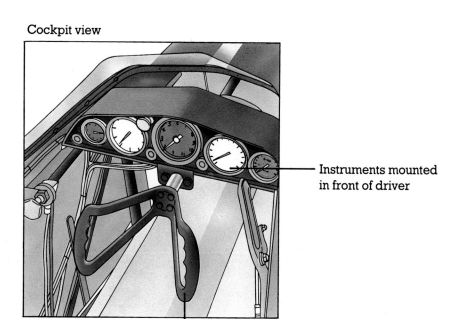

Instruments mounted
in front of driver

Steering wheel

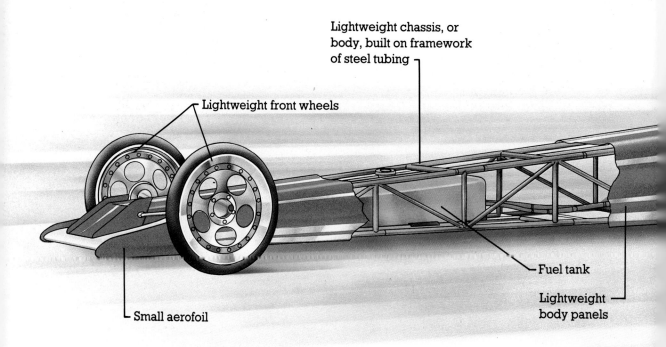

Lightweight chassis, or
body, built on framework
of steel tubing

Lightweight front wheels

Fuel tank

Lightweight
body panels

Small aerofoil

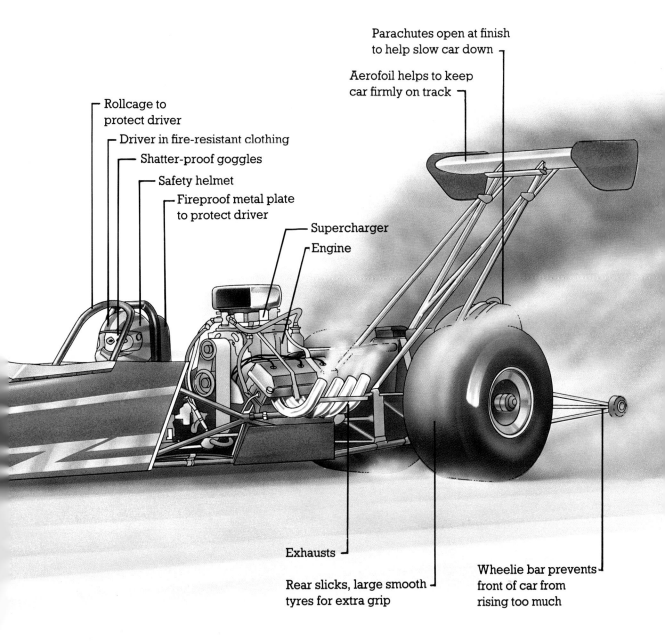

Parachutes open at finish
to help slow car down

Aerofoil helps to keep
car firmly on track

Rollcage to
protect driver

Driver in fire-resistant clothing

Shatter-proof goggles

Safety helmet

Fireproof metal plate
to protect driver

Supercharger

Engine

Exhausts

Rear slicks, large smooth
tyres for extra grip

Wheelie bar prevents
front of car from
rising too much

Drag racing

In drag racing, the winners of first-round races go through to the second round, while the losers are eliminated. Eventually, two cars are left to contest the final.

The drivers must not start until the lights change from amber to green. If a driver goes too soon, the red light on his or her side goes on and he or she is disqualified.

△ The set of signal lights used to start a drag race is called a Christmas tree. The cars line up behind a guard beam, between the two white boxes that can be seen to the left and right of the picture. If a driver breaks the beam before the lights change to green, the red light comes on.

A quick start is essential in drag racing. Drivers need fast reflexes, because races are won and lost by split seconds.

There is enormous acceleration, or increase in speed, at the start. It takes expert driving to keep a dragster under control. Terminal, or finishing, speeds of over 350 km/h (200 mph) are reached.

▽ At the end of a race, a parachute is released at the back of a dragster to help slow it down.

Most cars used in drag racing are built purely for competition. They cannot be driven on the roads. They are transported to and from the racetracks.

Dragster engines develop tremendous power. Drivers and mechanics are continually modifying their engines to get that little bit extra out of them, to make them go as fast as possible.

▷ The driver, sitting in front of the two huge back wheels, prepares to bring the bonnet down over the powerful engine of his funny car. He is firmly strapped in and wears a protective suit and helmet.

▽ A sleek top-fueller is carefully rolled out of its transporter.

Drag racing is a popular spectator sport. People enjoy the thrill of the racing and all the spectacular sights and sounds.

With such high speeds developed in such a short time, drag racing can also be dangerous. Engines may catch fire and there are crashes.

But there are now few serious accidents. Racetracks maintain a high standard of safety precautions for both drivers and spectators.

▽ There is always great activity in the pits, where mechanics and drivers tune their engines. Race fans can watch the action in the pits at close quarters, usually for an extra entrance fee.

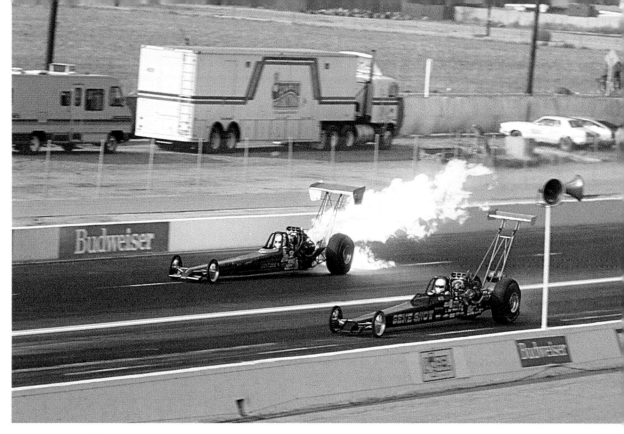

△ Drivers of top-fuellers are well protected if their engine catches fire. The engine is behind them, so the flames shoot back away from them. All drivers wear fire-resistant clothing.

▷ A wreck is towed off the track.

Top-fuellers

The low-slung, rear-engined top-fuel racers are the fastest dragsters. The leading drivers drive their cars along the quarter-mile strip in under six seconds.

Top-fuellers use a nitromethane fuel mixed with a small amount of methanol. They have supercharged engines, more powerful than any other racing car.

▽ The lights are green, and two top-fuellers roar across the starting line, front wheels already lifting off the ground.

Top-fuellers are the stars of drag racing. The leading drivers, especially in the United States, earn huge sums in prize money. But at this level, it is a very expensive sport. Top-fuel dragsters cost a fortune to build and run.

A similar class, called top-alcohol dragsters, run on methanol. They are not as fast as top-fuellers or funny cars.

△ Dense clouds of rubber smoke fill the air at a burnout as a driver warms up his back tyres. Burnouts may be done in a pool of water or a special liquid. The rubber of the tyres becomes sticky, and gives extra traction at the start.

▷ A front view of the start as two top-fuellers spring into action during a world championship event.

Spectators crowd the starting area, where some of the most exciting action is to be seen. They also enjoy the noise and the smells and the vibration of the ground as these powerful racing machines get under way.

Unlike circuit racing, where the starting and finishing lines are usually one and the same, the finish at drag racing is over 400 metres ($\frac{1}{4}$ mile) away. But a large scoreboard at the finish automatically lights up on the winner's side and can be seen clearly from the starting area.

Funny cars

Funny cars use the same engines and fuel as top-fuellers. But the engine of a funny car is mounted in front of the driver, in a shorter, stockier frame. It is covered by a fibreglass body.

Leading funny car drivers regularly clock times under six seconds, only fractionally slower than the best top-fuellers.

△ A beautifully turned out Corvette at a night meeting. Four of the eight exhausts can be seen sticking out under the fibreglass body.

The funny car class got its name because at one time these cars had such remarkable body modifications that they looked funny. Now the bodies are designed to look like current saloon cars.

Funny cars have a built-in rollbar for safety and the driver has a padded head restraint. Open cars are not permitted.

△ Track marshalls watch as two top alcohol funny cars cross the starting line. These cars are capable of times under seven seconds.

◁ A funny car flashes down the track in a blur of action, smoke billowing from its rear tyres.

Only the body resembles a production car. But it is smoothed and shaped to increase speed. The large rear wheels and high aerofoil give the car a steep appearance, or body rake. Sticking up through the bonnet, in front of the windscreen, is the top of the supercharger.

Other classes

◁ An "altered" Model-T Ford. A car in this class must have a body originally produced by a manufacturer or a replica of one. Few altereds, however, finish up looking anything like production cars.

▽ An altered Opel GT. At the back is a "wheelie" bar. This stops the front of the car lifting up too much.

△ The start of a pro
stock race. This is a
professional class for
unsupercharged cars
running on petrol. The
body must resemble
that of a standard
production car not more
than three or four years
old.

▷ Super gas cars also
run on petrol. This is an
amateur class. There
are no limits to the
modifications that may
be made, but there is a
minimum elapsed time
of 9.9 seconds.

△ It looks as if the super stock on the right has made a bad start, but this is a handicap race. This car has an allotted elapsed time, or e.t., of 9.65 seconds. Each car gets a separate green light, according to its e.t. But if a car betters its e.t., it is eliminated.

◁ All kinds of vehicles take part in drag racing, including vans and trucks.

Exhibitions

△ Special jet-powered dragsters provide an exciting spectacle for the crowd before the start of a meeting.

▷ Other forms of amusement at drag meets include the "wheelie" cars. They usually just give exhibitions, but sometimes a pair might race the full length of the track on their back wheels.

The story of dragsters

The first drag races

No one knows for sure exactly when drag racing began. But it was in California, probably in the 1920s. Motoring enthusiasts modified their cars to increase their top speed. They tested their speed over a measured quarter-mile on a dry lake bed. Regular meetings were held, where drivers put Model A and T Fords through their paces.

△ Early dragsters, called "slingshots", had the engine in front of the driver. The rear-mounted engine was introduced in the 1970s.

"Hot-rodders"

Hot-rodding became very popular in the US in the late 1940s. Thousands of ex-servicemen used mechanical skills acquired in World War II to build hot-rods. These are cars stripped down and modified for speed and power. Friendly competition took the form of drag races in the streets. This was very dangerous, as rival hot-rodders would accelerate away from the traffic lights with screeching tyres and in clouds of smoke.

To get drag racing off the streets, local airstrips were converted for use by hot-rodders. The first official meeting was staged in 1950 at a former naval base near Santa Ana, in California, where hot-rodders competed against motorcycles. The National Hot Rod Association (NHRA) was formed in the early 1950s to govern the sport in the US. The first national championships were held at Great Bend, Kansas, in 1955.

△ An early drag racing machine from the Don Garlits Museum, his first "Swamp Rat".

More power

As the sport grew, dragsters became more powerful. Instead of using modified vehicles, the top drag racers designed dragsters especially for the sport. They built them round the new powerful V8 engines being manufactured. Even aero-engines were tried and owners experimented with chemical fuel mixtures such as methanol, or methyl alcohol.

△ Some drag meets include a class for motorcycles. These streamlined models are very different from the bikes that competed against the first dragsters in the early 1950s.

More speed

Other improvements included the replacement of regular road tyres with "slicks". These are smooth, wide tyres that provide extra traction. To reduce weight, bodywork was kept to a minimum. Anything that was not essential was removed, including suspension and sometimes the gearbox. As a result, top speeds shot up. They rose from 150 mph (214 km/h) in 1955 to 200 mph (322 km/h) in 1964.

Drag racing goes international

Drag racing is still chiefly a US sport. But there are pockets of enthusiasts in other countries, especially Britain, where the first dragsters were motorcycles. A tour of Britain by the top US stars in 1964 helped to popularize the sport and it then spread to other countries.

Women in the sport

In motor sport, men and women compete on equal terms. Although women are considerably outnumbered by men in drag racing, they have produced some of the top stars. The most outstanding has been Shirley Muldowney, who in the 1980s became the first top-fueller – man or woman – to win the world championship three times.

△ Shirley Muldowney, triple world champion, made a comeback in January 1986 after a crash that nearly cost her her life 19 months earlier.

Facts and records

Quickest

At the top level, elapsed time (e.t.) is measured in thousandths of a second. Every now and then, someone knocks a few thousandths off a record. In October 1983, Californian Gary Beck became the first drag racer to break 5.4 seconds, when he recorded a time of 5.391 seconds in his top-fueller.

△ Gary Beck, the first racer to break 5.4 seconds.

High speed, low pressure

Racing slicks, the large, soft tyres used on dragsters, have an inner tyre and an outer casing. The inner tyre is well inflated, but the outer casing's pressure is a fraction of that used for tyres of road vehicles. Its pressure is only about 0.3 kg/sq cm (4 lb/sq in), compared with say 2 kg (30 lb) for a family saloon.

Daddy of drag racing

Don "Big Daddy" Garlits of Ocala, Florida, has broken countless records over the years and earned more prize money than anyone else in the sport. In October 1985 he set a record terminal speed of 431.31 km/h (268.01 mph).

△ Don Garlits, the biggest money winner in drag racing.

Glossary

Acceleration
The rate of change of speed.

Altered
A car based on an original body or a replica of one.

Burnout
This is carried out before the start to warm up a car's rear tyres and also to lay a film of rubber on the track to increase traction at the start. The rear wheels are spun in water or a special chemical.

Dragster
Any car used for drag racing, but usually meaning a top-fueller.

Elapsed time
The time for a car to complete the quarter-mile.

Fibreglass
A tough plastic.

Funny car
A class of cars with fibreglass bodies and front-mounted engines.

Hot-rod
A production car that has been stripped down and modified to make it faster.

Nitromethane
A type of rocket fuel used by top-fuellers and funny cars.

Pro stock
A class for cars resembling recent production models. They run on petrol and are not supercharged.

Slicks
Smooth, wide tyres.

Super gas
A class of car that runs on petrol and has a maximum allowed elapsed time of 9.9 seconds.

Super stock
A class for slightly modified production cars.

Terminal speed
The speed of a dragster measured at the finish.

Top-fueller
The fastest class of dragster.

Traction
Pulling power transmitted from the tyres to the track.

Wheelie bar
A device at the back of a car that prevents it rearing up.

Index